THE
BEAUTY
BOOK

Other Books Available

The Lily Series
  Here's Lily!
  Lily Robbins, M.D. (Medical Dabbler)
  Lily and the Creep
  Lily's Ultimate Party
  Ask Lily
  Lily the Rebel
  Lights, Action, Lily!
  Lily Rules!
  Rough & Rugged Lily
  Lily Speaks!
  Horse Crazy Lily
  Lily's Church Camp Adventure
  Lily's Passport to Paris
  Lily's in London?!

Nonfiction
  The Beauty Book
  The Body Book
  The Buddy Book
  The Best Bash Book
  The Blurry Rules Book
  The It's MY Life Book
  The Creativity Book
  The Uniquely Me Book
  The Year 'Round Holiday Book
  The Values & Virtues Book
  The Fun-Finder Book
  The Walk-the-Walk Book
  Dear Diary
  Girlz Want to Know
  NIV Young Women of Faith Bible
  Hey! This Is Me Journal
  Take It from Me

THE BEAUTY BOOK

it's a God thing!

Written by Nancy Rue
Illustrated by Steven Mach

zonder**kidz**

The children's group of Zondervan

www.zonderkidz.com

The Beauty Book
Copyright © 2000 by Women of Faith
Illustrations Copyright © 2000 by Steven Mach

Requests for information should be addressed to:
Grand Rapids, Michigan 49530

ISBN-10: 0-310-70014-0
ISBN-13: 978-0-310-70014-2

All Scripture quotations, unless otherwise indicated, are taken from the *Holy Bible: New International Version*®. NIV®. Copyright © 1973, 1978, 1984 by International Bible Society. Used by permission of Zondervan. All rights reserved.

Zonderkidz is a trademark of Zondervan.

Published in association with the literary agency of Alive Communications, Inc., 7680 Goddard Street, Suite 200, Colorado Springs, CO 80920.

Art direction and interior design by Michelle Lenger

Printed in the United States of America

05 06 07 08 /DCI/ 24 23 22

Contents

Ya Gotta Love It

LORD, you are our Father.
We are the clay, you are the potter;
we are all the work of your hand.

Isaiah 64:8

Ya Gotta Love It

Okay, let's get one fact straight right up front: Every girl has her own special beauty.

Yeah, I know you've heard your mother say, "Well, *I* think you're beautiful, honey." I also know that doesn't mean a whole bunch when some kid's calling you "Pizza Face," or everybody's telling your sister she's drop-dead gorgeous and then patting you on the head and saying, "You're cute, too, dear."

But really, God doesn't make junk. He made each of us just exactly the way he intends us to be. So just like everything else God made—from blackberries to rhinoceroses—*ya gotta love it*. Ya gotta love *you*, too.

Yeah, you may ask, but if every girl is beautiful, how come "everybody" isn't seeing it that way?

Because—bummer!—people aren't like God. Somewhere along the way, since the whole Adam and Eve thing, somebody decided there was only one way to be a beautiful woman at any given time. Right now it's being five-foot–ten, weighing about a hundred pounds, and having lips as big as the living-room couch.

So how are you supposed to convince "everybody" that you're this knockout, even though God shaped you like a fire hydrant and gave you lips the width of a pencil line?

You aren't. You only need to convince *yourself*, and that's what this book is about. By the time you get to the end, I want you to be able to check yourself out when you pass a store window and say, "That's me. Cool! Ya gotta love that!"

Here's a good way to start. From now until you finish reading this book, try to follow this rule: NO DISSING THE WAY YOU LOOK!

That means no dwelling on the zits that have appeared on your forehead. No talking about how fat you are. No wishing you had curlier hair (or smaller ears or straighter teeth). Pretend you are a friend of yours, and you would

rather eat Brussels sprouts than hurt that friend's feelings. NO putting your friend—you!—down.

That's a really hard rule to follow, so let's look at some of the things that can keep you from seeing how gorgeous you are.

BEAUTY BLOCKER #1: TV Training

One of the reasons people think there's only one way to be beautiful is because that's all they see on television and in magazines and movies and on billboards. Even the Barbie dolls seem to scream, "You have to look like me!" But you don't!

Girlz WANT TO KNOW

✿ *LILY: Those girls on the cover of Seventeen have perfect skin. How do they get that?*

They don't. Nobody's skin is *that* perfect. Everybody has at least the occasional zit, freckle, or scar from when she had the chicken pox. Those magazine photos are doctored up and retouched with computers that can remove blemishes, make eyelashes longer, and even give people great cheekbones! If you met those models in person, you would see that they have pimples, birthmarks, and little scars, too. No lie!

✿ *ZOOEY: If I use those shampoos and face creams I see in the ads, will I look the way the models do?*

Probably not. For openers, that model isn't you. And don't you think if a company wants to sell a product that's supposed to give you thick, shiny hair, they're going to pick somebody who already has that thick, shiny hair? Besides, if you were born with thin hair, there isn't much in this world that's going to make it thick. But who says you have to have thick hair to be beautiful?

✿ *RENI: I'm the shrimpiest girl in my whole class. How come God even makes short girls, when tall girls are always the ones people think are beautiful?*

Actually, people's ideas of what's beautiful change over time, thanks to "the media." Back in the late 1500s and early 1600s, plump women with rolls of rosy flesh were considered beautiful, mostly because the better-fed you were, the wealthier you were. In the 1950s, lots of curves were the going thing in the movies and on the posters. By today's standards, Marilyn Monroe would have been considered overweight, but men in the '50s drooled over full-figured women. In the 1960s when the Beatles said on the radio that they preferred petite girls, everybody wanted to be a short little peanut. The Beach Boys even had a line in a song that went, "You're kinda small and you're such a doll. I'm glad you're mine."

Does that mean somebody who *was* beautiful 40, 50, or 400 years ago *wouldn't* be beautiful today? How much sense does *that* make? Nah, *this* makes sense: Everyone has beauty—plump and rosy, round and curvy, short and pixie-like, *and* tall and pencil slim—not to mention everything in between.

BEAUTY BLOCKER #2: The Comparison Game

Come on, we've all played it.

"I don't have breasts yet, so I'm not as grown-up as Stephanie, but at least I don't have to wear those geeky braces like Whitney, so I can't be *that* bad."

It seems like a harmless enough game. After all, most of the time you just play it in your mind until you come out ahead of somebody and can make yourself feel better, right? Well . . . hmm. Let's see what God has to say about that.

HOW IS THIS A God Thing?

The question "What would Jesus do?" is everywhere these days, on bracelets and license plates, and it's even been spotted on boxer shorts, for Pete's sake. But what *would* Jesus do when faced with the temptation to make himself feel like he was okay by playing the comparison game? Would he say to himself, "Yikes, I don't have big muscles like Peter, so I must be pretty wimpy. Still, he's always asking stupid questions. I gotta be smarter than him. That's more important, right, Dad?"

Pretty lame. And if it's too lame for Jesus, it's too lame for us. Dad, uh, God certainly doesn't compare us. Can you imagine him saying, "I sure did a great job on Carly's complexion. Too bad I messed up on Emily's. She's not nearly as cute." *Hello!*

God doesn't compare us. Jesus doesn't compare us. The world we live in compares us, but who are we supposed to follow?

Jesus made it really plain. Love your neighbor as yourself. That means no putting your "neighbor" down, and no putting yourself down. Period.

✓ CHECK Yourself OUT

Each statement below has four possible endings. Circle the number next to the ending that fits you *best* in each group. Be *honest*. No fair picking the answer you think is "right." (What would you learn from that?)

A. When it comes to height in my class,
- 4 I know right off the bat exactly how many people are taller and how many people are shorter than me.
- 3 I'd have to think about where I fall.
- 2 I couldn't figure it out if you paid me.
- 1 I don't care.

B. If you're talking complexion,
- 4 I have one of the best (or worst) in the class.
- 3 Now that you mention it, I do know how mine compares to other people's in my class.
- 2 I don't know—I never thought about it.
- 1 I don't *want* to think about it.

C. When I think about hair,

   4   I know I have more (or less) bad hair days than most people in my class.

   3   Well ... hmm ... let me think.

   2   Do people in my class have hair?

   1   Who *cares* about other people's hair?

D. If somebody brought a scale to class,

   4   I'd weigh bunches more (or less) than anybody else; I'm sure of it.

   3   I guess I know where I'd fall, but I'd have to see everybody else's weight written down.

   2   Why? Is somebody fat or something?

   1   Don't know, don't care.

E. Can we talk—about chests?

   4   I'm convinced I have the biggest (or smallest) one in class.

   3   Come to think of it, I guess mine is one of the bigger (or smaller, or average) ones in class.

   2   I'd have to get out a tape measure.

   1   I care about this because ... ?

F. Spastic? Clumsy? Me?

   4   I'm the most (or least) spastic person in the class. I don't even have to think about it.

   3   It's not something I think about a whole lot, but, yeah, I fit onto the spastic scale somewhere.

   2   What's a spastic?

   1   Why are we even *talking* about this?

G. If I had to rate myself for overall appearance in comparison to my classmates,

   4   I would put myself way at the top (or bottom) of the list without a second thought.

   3   Gee, if I really put my mind to it I could probably decide.

   2   I guess it all depends on what you consider beautiful.

   1   I have better things to do.

Now add up your points. Then read what you've just discovered about yourself.

If you scored between 28 and 22 points, you qualify for the Olympic Comparison Games! You may be making yourself unhappy by constantly measuring yourself against other people. Next time you feel yourself doing that, try paying that person you're comparing yourself to a compliment, then thank God for what you look like, and move on!

If you scored between 21 and 15 points, you are an amateur at the comparison game, but you'll play if somebody suggests it. Have you had conversations like this?

YOUR FRIEND: Do you think Susie Shmo is prettier than me?

YOU: No way! Her teeth are way bigger than yours and besides, she has a pig nose.

If you find yourself being pulled into that, you might want to have an answer ready for keeping yourself out, like this:

YOUR FRIEND: Do you think Susie Schmo is prettier than me?

YOU: I don't play that game. Monopoly, checkers, those I'll play.

WARNING: Your friend will probably think you're trying to dodge the "truth" that Susie Schmo really *is* prettier than she is, but you can get *that* out of her head by paying her a compliment that doesn't compare her to Susie or anybody else. Something like this:

YOUR FRIEND: So you *do* think she's prettier than me?

YOU: Your hair is amazing—you've got a smile to die for— yikes, the dimples, girl, the dimples.

She'll have forgotten all about Susie Schmo by that time!

If you scored between 14 and 18, you're probably baffled by all this talk of comparing. It just doesn't occur to you to compare people's appearances, and you wouldn't know where to start if it did. Be glad, but be careful. People, even your friends, may try to drag you into it:

YOUR FRIEND: Do you think Susie Schmo is prettier than me?

YOU: Huh?

YOUR FRIEND: Susie Schmo. Do you think she has better hair than me?

YOU: Hair? I don't know. I never thought about it.
YOUR FRIEND: Well, think about it!

And what comes next?

YOU: Nope. Sorry. That's not my thing.

If you scored a 7, congratulations! You not only don't compare people's beauty, but it really ticks you off when other people do it and try to make you do it. Keep it up. God likes that about you.

BEAUTY BLOCKER #3: The Teaser

Whether it's your little brother, your Uncle Charlie, or those girls at the other end of your lunch table, if somebody teases you about the way you look, it can twist your image of yourself. Even when you know the person is "just kidding" and says, "Dude—can't you take a joke?" stuff like this can hurt:

"Hey, Jody, when's the Breast Fairy going to come visit you?"

"Yikes, Sarah, with feet like that, who needs swim fins, right?"

"How you doin', Chubby?"

Maybe you usually give one of these answers to teasing:

"I'm just glad I don't have a chest like *yours,* Dolly Parton!"

"I don't have big feet! What are you talking about?"

"Oh, shut up!"

But none of those helps you with your image of yourself and your own beauty. God, as usual, has a better way to deal with teasing.

HOW IS THIS A God Thing?

It's spelled out right in the Bible!

A person who teases you is at that moment what Proverbs calls "a fool." He or she is the one who ought to be embarrassed, not you!

Fools are leaky faucets, dripping nonsense.
(Prov. 15:2 The Message)

All they do is run off at the mouth.
(Prov. 18:2 The Message)

Don't try to argue with a teaser.

**Don't bother talking sense to fools; They'll only poke
fun at your words.**
(Prov. 23:9 The Message)

Don't join in, either. You're just as much of a "fool" if you tease back.

The start of a quarrel is like a leak in a dam, so stop it before it bursts.
(Prov. 17:14 The Message)

And for Pete's sake, don't get mad and turn it into a fight.

**A gentle response defuses anger but a sharp tongue
kindles a temper fire.**
(Prov. 15:1 The Message)

Let teasers who aren't friends or family know you think they're fools—by ignoring them.

**Don't respond to the stupidity of fools;
You'll only look foolish yourself.**

(Prov. 26:4 The Message)

If it's someone in your family or a close friend, tell that person that teasing hurts you. Honesty is always best in a relationship. You can tell them

**Words kill, words give life, they're either poison or
friend—you choose.**
(Prov. 18:21 The Message)

Try to remember this about teasing: It just flat out isn't *true!*

**You have as little to fear from an undeserved curse as from the
dart of a wren or the swoop of a swallow.**
(Prov. 26:2 The Message)

By the way, if *you* are a teaser, remember this:

If you are dumb enough to call attention to yourself by offending people, don't be surprised if someone bloodies your nose!
(Prov. 30:32 The Message)

FINDING THE You-Nique You

Now that we've talked about what *not* to do—

don't be influenced by the media

don't play the Comparison Game

don't let teasing twist your mind

Let's talk about what you *can* do to get the right picture of your own beauty in your mind. How do you believe you are the beautiful young woman God made you to be when everyone else is telling you you're *not*?

You do it by discovering that special beauty. You figure out what is UNIQUE about your appearance—what makes you one of a kind—what makes you *you*.

Let's go on a search for the "You-nique You."

CHECK Yourself OUT

Take this quiz in front of the biggest mirror you can find. While looking at yourself in the mirror and remembering that the girl you see there is your friend, complete the sentences below. There are two rules for your answers.

RULE #1: Your answer has to be honest.
RULE #2: Your answer has to be a compliment.

Example:
Her hair is the stringiest stuff on the planet. (NO!)
Her hair is long and wispy and soft. (YES!)

Are you in front of your mirror? Here we go. Remember, you're writing about *yourself*.

Her (that's you!) hair is_____

Her forehead is _____

Her ears are _____

Her eyebrows are _____

Her eyes are _____

Her nose is _____

Her complexion is _____

Her cheeks are _____

Her mouth is _____

Her smile is _____

Her chin is _____

Her height is _____

Her arms are _____

Her legs are _____

Now read your statements out loud, one after the other, as if you're reading about a character in a book, or, better yet, about your friend.

Try to come up with one statement that describes this whole You. Like

This girl sounds cute, like a little elf with wonderful big ears!
OR
This girl is a round, healthy, wholesome looking angel!
This girl (YOU!) _____.

Just Do It

Now your job is to believe that—every day, all the time. You are uniquely beautiful in the way you've just described. You didn't make it up—it was there right in front of you. Try one of these ways to help yourself *know* that it's true:

Keep your description of yourself in a place where you can read it often (and where your brother can't get hold of it!).

Are you artistic? Draw a picture of "this girl" following your written description exactly. Keep your drawing where you can see *you* often.

Every time you hear yourself saying or thinking, "My legs are so fat," toss that thought out and replace it with something you wrote, such as *My legs are really smooth.*

When you pray, thank God, item by item, for the *you* you've described: "Thank you, Father, for my chocolate-fudge brown eyes and my two big front teeth that make me look like a cute bunny and my long thin arms that will probably never be flabby." God wants to know that you appreciate everything he's done for you.

God-CONFIDENCE

Now that you're starting to be convinced that you *are* beautiful, let's look at another very important part of this.

Have you ever known a girl who looked like she just came off the cover of *Seventeen*? One who never had to worry about anyone saying, "My hair (or anything else!) looks better than hers?" Who was never teased about any part of her whole self?

And—who was so hateful sometimes that she was downright ugly to look at?

Have you ever known a girl who maybe had some big-time funky things about her appearance—maybe she was cross-eyed or had buck teeth? But the more you got to know her, the prettier she seemed because not only was she nice to everyone but she was nice to herself, as well?

The reason? It's true. You do look good when you *are* good. You look beautiful when you are sure of yourself. A lot of people call that *self-confidence.* It's really *God-confidence.*

CHECK Yourself OUT

See for yourself. Get in front of that mirror again. Smile at that girl as if you like her and accept her and want to be best friends. Now watch what happens when you look at her as if you hate her guts. Which girl looks better?

How Is This a God Thing?

You can have that God-confidence that makes you beautiful because

- God carefully chose each of your features and combined them to make *you*.
- God's idea of you is perfect, even if the going look for models doesn't agree.
- Jesus talked only about inner beauty, and if you got him, you've got that, baby!

Now think about *that* and look in the mirror! You gotta love that!

Talking to God About It

If you're like most girls, what we've talked about in this chapter is a lot of new stuff, some really different ways of thinking about *you*. How are you ever going to remember it all?

Relax! You don't have to do it on your own. That's what God's there for, to help you. All you have to do is ask.

Write a prayer about the things you want to remember about being the You-Nique, Beautiful You. Fill in the blanks below if you want, or write your own prayer.

Dear _____, (your favorite name for God)

I'm just discovering I'm beautiful because you made me that way. But sometimes it's hard for me to remember and believe that because _____. I especially have a hard time thinking of my_____ as beautiful. Will you please help me not to pay attention to what TV and magazines say is beautiful, especially _____.
Will you please help me not to play the Comparison Game, especially about or with _____. And, Lord, please help me to deal with _____'s teasing about my _____. Most of all,

God, help me to remember that you love me, that you made me per-fect, that I can have the God-confidence that makes me You-niquely different from everyone else.

I love you, God! _____

Lily Pad

The time I felt the absolute prettiest was when...

Heads Up!

**Even the very hairs of your head
are all numbered.**

Matthew 10:30

How Is Hair a God Thing?

One of the things God wants us to do is make the very most of what he's given us. You are the *most* beautiful when you're taking care of your temple—that's your physical self.

What better place to start than with your hair, because if that crowning glory isn't glorious, you aren't going to feel as beautiful as you truly are.

Here's to Your Hair Health

Before we even *think* about curling irons and body perms and French braids, we have to talk about healthy hair. If your hair's "sick," it isn't going to look great no matter what else you do to it.

Just Do It

Take a look at your hair habits. Answer these questions and, of course, be honest.

1. How often do you wash your hair?

Your hair might be starting to look "greasier" as you're getting older because the glands that produce oil are making more of it now. The best guideline is to wash your hair whenever it starts to look stringy or feel oily. For most girls that's several times a week. For *way* active girls and those with lots of oil, every day is good.

2. What kind of shampoo do you use? Is it made especially for your hair type (dry, normal, oily, fine)? (Check the label.)

It should be!

Is it PH-balanced?

It should be!

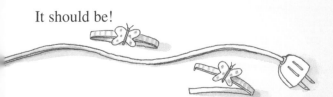

3. How much shampoo do you use?

A "serving" about the size of a quarter in the palm of your hand is a good guideline.

4. Do you get all the tangles out of your hair before you wash it?

You should!

5. How do you scrub your hair?

After you've spread your 25-cent-size helping of shampoo evenly over your wet hair, work it in all the way to your roots, but don't scratch at your scalp with your fingernails. Massage with your fingertips.

Scrub harder—but still don't "scratch"—around your whole hairline. If your hair is really oily, be extra gentle with the massage so you don't get your oil glands working overtime.

6. Do you rinse your hair until there's no more soap coming out of it?

Soap left in your hair will make it dry and dull. They say rinsing with cold water—if you can stand it!—will really give your hair body.

7. Do you use conditioner on your hair?

Not everybody needs to. Use conditioner if

- your hair gets really tangled when you wash it;
- your hair is very dry;

- your hair's been damaged, maybe from a perm or using hot rollers, curling irons, or blow dryers a lot.

8. How much conditioner do you use?

Use just enough to put on the ends of your hair. If you use too much, your hair will be limp and so soft you won't be able to do fun things with it.

9. How often do you have your hair cut or trimmed?

If you answered, "Never! I want my hair to grow *way* long!" or "I don't know; whenever it starts to look stupid, I guess," you might want to know this—it's best to have your hair trimmed every four to six weeks to get rid of the split ends. If you want long, healthy hair, get a trim on schedule and it will grow. If it's a bunch of split ends, it'll never get longer. Honest. Anybody's hair can be healthy, and healthy hair means you'll have your own personal bounce and shine.

You've Got Style, Girl!

Remember when we talked about the You-Nique You? That really applies to the hairdo you choose. A style you like on somebody else might not be the best one for you. But there is one that's perfect for you.

Check Yourself OUT

Check the answer under each statement that best describes you.

1. **When I run my hands through my hair, it feels**
   - ○ Thin and fine
   - ○ Sort of medium
   - ○ Thick
   - ○ I can't run my hands through my hair!

Be sure your hair can do what you're asking it to do. A way thick mane of tight, curly hair isn't going to cascade down your back, and very fine hair just won't be happy in a French braid!

2. My personality (most of the time) is
- ☐ Bubbly
- ☐ Mature for my age
- ☐ Dreamy and quiet
- ☐ Sporty
- ☐ Artistic
- ☐ Studious

Be sure the 'do you're thinking about is "you." Are you going for little curls all around your face when a sleek ponytail matches your let's-play-soccer personality? That doesn't mean you can't "try on" different "you's," but for your everyday usual 'do, you'll want to be comfortable under your hair.

3. The way I live is
- ○ I have a lot of free time
- ○ I'm pretty busy, but I'm really active
- ○ I'm super busy
- ○ I'm not active physically like a tornado

Make sure your hairdo matches your lifestyle. Do you have time to blow-dry and use hot rollers every day? Do you have to be able to keep the hair out of your face for gymnastics or soccer or dance class?

4. I would best describe my body as
- ☐ Tiny and pixie-like. (Beware of too-big hair that wears you!)
- ☐ Short, round, and cuddly. (Don't let your hair be round, too, or you will get lost in there!)
- ☐ Somewhere in the middle. (Nothing too extreme is best.)
- ☐ Tall and willowy. (Try not to let your hair be droopy.)
- ☐ Like a big, wonderful teddy bear. (Steer away from busy 'dos or those cut really close to your head.)
- ☐ Sturdy, strong, and powerfully square. (Best not to wear your hair too severe; go soft.)

Now brush your hair back so you can see the shape and size of your face. If it's okay with the grown-ups, use the corner of a bar of soap to trace that shape on a mirror.

5. **Is the shape you've drawn**
   - ○ **Round?** Long and straight works with your wonderfully soft face. So does some height on top and fullness at the sides. Short and curly can be fun, but just know that it will give you a cherub look.
   - ○ **Square?** How classy! Make the most of that very sophisticated face-shape with your hair cut either above or below your jawline but not right at it. Nothing too foofy at the corners of your forehead or jaw-line, either.
   - ○ **Long?** A long face is so dramatic and exotic. You won't want to pile hair up on top of your head, but go ahead and puff it out at the sides.
   - ○ **Triangle or pear-shaped?** That's a face with interest and character! Experiment with different types of bangs. Play with angles, but keep it smooth at your jawline.
   - ○ **Heart-shaped?** How romantic! Curls or fluffiness at your jawline is perfect. You won't want a lot of puff on top, though.
   - ○ **Oval?** Just about anything goes for you. Have a ball. Try new things. You can hardly go wrong.

Things to Remember When You're Stylin'

- Never brush wet hair because it will break easily. Use a wide tooth comb to get out tangles, and don't go after them like you're raking the lawn! Start with the ends and slowly work your way up.
- Use a brush with round tips on the bristles. Natural bristles are the easiest on your hair.
- Wash your brush and comb once a week in—what else?—shampoo!
- Don't share combs and brushes. It's kind of like lending or borrowing a toothbrush!
- Blow-dryers, curling irons, and hot rollers can really dry out your hair and leave you with a head full of frizzy straw. Use your blow-dryer on the lowest setting, and try not to use curling irons or hot rollers every day.
- Mousse is good for giving your hair body if it's thin and fine, but use just a little bit. If you put it on like whipped cream, your hair will look stiff.

- Gel is fun for "special effects" when you don't care if your hair looks "fixed" or stiff.
- Hair spray keeps your hair from flying all over the place, but again, a little goes a long way. It can take the shine out of your hair.

Hair Hassles
Girlz WANT TO KNOW

✿   *SUZIE: I swim in a pool almost every day. Is the chlorine bad for my hair? Will it turn green?*

Chlorine will give blonde hair a greenish tint. It can also dry out anybody's hair. Here are some tips to help:

- Wet your hair with clear water before you get into the pool. Wet hair absorbs less chlorine.
- Rinse the chlorine out of your hair right after you've finished swimming.
- Regular shampoo works just as well as special shampoos made for swimmers.

✿   *KRESHA: I keep getting white flakes on my shoulders from my hair. Gross! What are they?*

If your scalp feels dry and itchy, you might have *dandruff*, which is not gross. It's just a common condition you can get rid of by using a special dandruff shampoo from the drugstore or from your doctor. Before you try a dandruff shampoo, though, ask yourself if you've been using a lot of mousse, hair spray, or gel and haven't washed your hair every day. Those products can build up and cause itching and flakes that will go away with regular shampooing.

❁ *LILY: My little brother thought he'd be cute and stick gum in my hair. How do I get that out?*

Spread some peanut butter on that wad o' gum and work it through until the gum comes out. Then wash the peanut butter out of your hair, of course!

❁ *ZOOEY: My hair is, like, falling out! Every time I brush it I get all this hair left in my brush! Am I going to go bald?*

You can probably relax—and you should, since you lose less hair when you're relaxed. Most people lose about a hundred hairs a day. Since you have about 100,000 hairs growing from your scalp, you'll still have plenty at the end of the day! Of course, if you notice actual bald spots, tell a grown-up.

❁ *RENI: I'm African-American, you know, and my hair just breaks all the time.*

God made black girls' hair especially fragile. Try not to use picks or other sharp tools. If you use a straightener or a curl-relaxer, always use a conditioner afterward. Have your mom give you a hot oil treatment now and then.

Talking to God ABOUT IT: Hair Prayer

I can almost hear you saying, "Does God really want to talk about my hair?"

God wants to talk about anything that stands between you and him and anything that makes you the *you* he has in mind. That includes your hair.

So as you get ready to pray today, check the subjects below that you—the You-Nique You—want to talk with God about. Of course, add any I've left out—and use your own words to go to God with what's on your mind (or on your hair!).

I want to talk to God about

- the way I feel about my hair. I still think it's ugly, and I know that's wrong.
- the fact that I stress way too much about my hair. I have a bad hair day and I freak out.
- my not caring how I look. I forget to comb my hair half the time or I fight with my mom about washing it or getting it cut.
- how my mom won't let me wear my hair the way I want. I know I'm supposed to honor my parents, but—help!
- being thankful for every hair on my head, just the way it is!

Lily Pad

If God talked to me about my hair, I bet he'd say…

The Skinny on Skin

**This is now ... flesh of my flesh;
she shall be called "woman."**
Genesis 2:23

It's Gotta Be Healthy

Next to your hair, your skin is the physical part of you that has to have the most care if you're going to be beautiful You-Nique You. That figures, since your skin is your body's biggest organ!

Girlz WANT TO KNOW

✿ *ZOOEY: My mom dragged me to this skin-care party, and the lady said we needed all these cleansers and toners and moisturizer thingies. I got so confused! Do I really need all that stuff?*

All you need to do right now is keep your face *clean*. Wash it when you get up and before you go to bed with a mild facial soap or facial cleanser. Don't use a deodorant bar or the body scrub you use for the rest of your body. Apply it with your hands or a soft washcloth. Rinse with warm—not hot!—water. That's all.

✿ *LILY: My skin is so white I blind people with it! I know the sun is bad for your skin but can't I just get a little tan to give me some color?*

Actually, no. What's wrong with white skin—or any other shade of skin God gave you? There is no such thing as a safe tan. Period. That's it. No buts. The sun (or a tanning bed) damages everybody's skin and can give you.

- early wrinkles
- brown spots
- burns
- allergic reactions
- skin cancer—and not just when you're "old"

32

❀ *LILY: Does that mean I'm never supposed to go out in the sun?*

No. The sun also provides vitamin D, which is very good for you. Just protect yourself:

- Wear sunscreen with an SPF (sun protection factor) of at least 15. That means it will protect your skin 15 times longer than if you don't use anything. Use it especially between ten in the morning and three in the afternoon, but to be on the safe side, use it all the time because the sun's rays are always dangerous, even when it's cloudy or cold.
- If you're out in the sun longer than a few hours, put on more sunscreen.
- Put on sunscreen again after you've been in the water. Every time!
- When you aren't swimming, cover up with a shirt and a hat.
- Go for the shade whenever you can.
- Don't feel like a wimp for protecting yourself. You're just making sure you won't end up looking like a piece of luggage or having skin cancer.

❀ *SUZIE: That's it? Just wash your face and stay out of the sun?*

Basically. And eat a healthy diet and get plenty of exercise and drink lots of water. If you're not sure what a healthy diet is or how much exercise is good, read The Body Book.

Face Flaws!

Just when you really start to care about how you look—bingo!—your skin breaks out and you feel like a pepperoni pizza. Or you get a big old cold sore that resembles a raspberry hanging on your lip. And nobody—but *nobody*—can convince you that *that* is beautiful!

Okay—so we deal with stuff like that. Here's how.

CHECK Yourself OUT

Wash your face and don't put lotions, creams, or makeup on it. Now get in front of that mirror again and take this "skin survey." Under each statement, circle the response that best fits the You-Nique You.

1. Let's talk zits. On my face I have
    a. No pimples at all.
    b. A couple of blackheads or pimples here and there.
    c. Some areas where I'm broken out.
    d. About a zillion zits all over!

If you answered

    a—You're lucky! Be prepared, though, okay? Pimples could happen anytime, because as you get older your body will produce more oil. That oil combines with bacteria to clog up your pores. Presto—pimples. Since you have 94 oil glands per square inch of skin, the number of possible zits boggles the mind!

    b—Don't freak. Everybody is going to get a blemish now and then. Keep your face clean and do *not* pick at or pop even one pimple. The oils and bacteria on your hands, no matter how clean your hands are, can turn an innocent whitehead into a big breakout and maybe even leave a scar. Leave the thing alone and it'll go away.

    c—Don't let it get to you. A breakout on one or two parts of your face is easy to prevent or at least improve. Besides keeping your face clean and your hands away from it (no pimple-popping!), think about what might be adding more oil to that part of your skin. If the breakout is on your forehead, your bangs might be the culprit. Keep your hair extra clean, don't use gels or sprays on your bangs, and perhaps get the hair off your face until it clears up. If you wear glasses, and pimples appear on the bridge of your nose, be sure to clean your specs daily. Chin zits? Check out your habits. Do you rest your chin in your hands when doing homework? Keep hands extra clean while trying to retrain yourself.

d—You are not a gross, disgusting, dirty person! You just have *acne*, which is a skin condition common in the preteen and teen years. You can't help it that you have it (even a family history of acne can contribute to it), but you can make it less painful for yourself.

• Keep your skin very clean, but don't scrub it hard. Scrubbing will only irritate your skin more.

• Try a special facial cleanser for acne that you can buy at a drugstore. Products that contain *benzyl peroxide* are good, but test some on the inside of your wrist before putting it on your face. If you get a rash on your wrist, don't use it on your face.

• If your acne really gets out of control—it's hurting and it's upsetting you—ask your mom or dad to take you to a *dermatologist* (skin doctor) who can prescribe special creams or pills.

• Remember that acne usually clears up in the late teen years. That seems like a long way away, but God'll help you through till then!

2. The skin on my lips is
   a. Smooth and soft.
   b. Dry and cracked.
   c. Plagued with a big old sore (or has been before).

If you answered

a—That's a blessing! Be sure to use lip balm with sunscreen when you spend a lot of time out in the sun. Lips burn, too.

b—Uncomfortable, huh? You can clear up chapped lips with lip balm in a tube or stick. While you're at it, you might as well use one with sunscreen in it. Drink at least six glasses of water a day. Your lips are telling you your body's dried out.

c—Bummer. You have (or have had) a cold sore, also called a fever blister. It's caused by a virus, sort of like chicken pox, that will zap you when you're sick or stressed. The drugstore will have products that should help. If they don't, ask your doctor to prescribe something stronger.

What About Makeup?

You might have seen some girls your age wearing lipstick and mascara and blush. Maybe you thought, "Dude! Isn't she a little young?" Or you might have thought, "Oh, am I supposed to be thinking about wearing makeup?" Or you may even have thought, "That looks good—I really want to start wearing it myself." Yikes—maybe you've even thought all of those things at the same time!

If we're going to talk about the You-Nique, Beautiful You, these questions are worth answering. Let's ask God.

HOW IS THIS A God Thing?

God comes into the makeup thing this way. He says, "Honor your father and your mother, so that you may live long in the land the LORD your God is giving you" (Exod. 20:12).

You have to live with your parents for a long time. If you want to live peacefully (and long!), you need to ask their permission about stuff like this!

Seriously, discuss when you'll be allowed to wear makeup with your mom and dad. Parents usually have some pretty good reasons for wanting their daughters to wait before they go for the lipstick and eyeliner. Some of them even go back to the Bible.

- They might think it looks "cheap." Remember Jezebel, the cheapest chick in the Bible (the one who had God's prophets bumped off)? She used to "paint her eyes." The "bad girls" of the Bible were often described as the ones who painted up their eyes to look sly. If it isn't done right, makeup can definitely make a girl look too sophisticated when she isn't.

- They don't want you to get all wrapped up in the whole appearance thing. Even the prophets, like Jeremiah, used to warn against spending so much time adorning yourself you forget what's important. In Esther chapter 2, you can read about the girls who were to be presented to the king spending six months learning how to use cosmetics!
- They don't want you to try to look older than you are. They'd rather you be just who you are right now. That's what God wants, too!

Listen to your parents' reasoning. If you disagree, it's okay to present your case calmly. But if you're ready to go for the gloss and the blush and they say no, remember that it isn't the end of life as you know it. You're a natural beauty. The "enhancing" of it that you do with makeup will come in time.

And no fair taking lipstick and powder to school and putting them on in the bathroom when your mom has already said no! Sneakiness doesn't look good on anybody!

A good compromise might be being allowed to experiment with makeup at home but not wear it out of the house. That way when it's time for public viewing, you'll be an expert.

If They Say Yes, Remember . . .

- Too much makeup is worse than none. Use makeup to draw attention to your natural beauty, not to try to change it.
- Get someone with experience to help you at first. It takes skill and practice to use makeup right. Otherwise, you could end up looking a lot like Ronald McDonald.
- Try one thing at a time. Maybe you'll be happy with just some lip gloss or a coat of mascara or some blush.

- Don't use makeup you don't need. If you have clear skin, who needs foundation? If your cheeks are naturally rosy, skip the blush.
- Have fun experimenting, but remember that you want people to see the real you—not your makeup!
- Always take makeup off after you're finished trying things or at the end of the day.
- Don't share makeup. That isn't stingy—it's just safe!

Fun Treats for Your Skin

Taking care of your skin doesn't have to be a drag. Try treating yourself to a "skin snack" once in a while—with a grown-up's permission, of course. Here are some fun ones to try. Your mom might even want to do one with you!

Just Do It

- Mix natural yogurt with lemon juice and spread it on your skin. This one is good for ALL your skin, not just your face. Lie back and relax for a while!
  - Use a base of yogurt and lemon juice, and spread it over your face. Then cover all but your lips and eyes with sliced strawberries, cucumber, or tomatoes! It's sure to give you the giggles, but your skin will feel great after fifteen or twenty minutes.
    - Soak a washcloth or small towel in hot water, wring it out, and place it over your face. Repeat this until your skin starts to glow.

Talking to God About It

When you pray today, why not talk to God about your skin stuff? He wants to share everything with you—even your zit woes and your freckle freak-outs. Just spill it all out, or use this little guide.

God? It's me again. I just want to talk to you about
Taking care of this big ol' organ, my skin:

_____

_____

_____

_____

Dealing with zits:

_____

_____

_____

_____

The whole staying-out-of-the-sun thing:

_____

_____

_____

_____

The makeup issue:

_____

_____

_____

_____

Other skin stuff:

_____

_____

_____

Thanks for the skin you gave me, especially:

_____

_____

_____

Lily Pad

Can you imagine yourself as an old lady with wrinkly skin? What do you think you'll look like?

Hands 'n' Feet

How beautiful on the mountains are the
feet of those who bring good news.

Isaiah 52:7

Everyone who believes in me will be able to
do wonderful things. ... They will heal sick
people by placing their hands on them.

Mark 16:17–18

Your hands and feet are two of the instruments God uses most. Naturally, then, they're part of the You-Nique Beautiful You.

Girlz WANT TO KNOW

✿ *ZOOEY: I already have to take care of my hair and my skin. Now I have to worry about my hands and feet, too?*

No worries! Hands and feet are easy to pamper. There are just a couple of things you'll need to do regularly:

- Give yourself a manicure once a week and a pedicure every other week, even if it's just cleaning and clipping and filing. You can do it while you're listening to music or talking on the phone or watching a good video.
- Use moisturizing lotion on your hands and feet after you take a shower or bath. Even young skin can dry out on those places you use so much!

It's a piece o' cake!

♣ *LILY: It really matters what my hands and feet look like?*

Sure. Have you ever seen a girl with great hair, good skin, and terrific clothes—then you looked down at her hands and saw that her nails were chipped and chewed or her skin was chapped? Or have you ever been to the beach with a friend who took all kinds of care with the beach 'do and the right swimsuit, but had grimy feet or hard heels? It isn't the end of the world, of course, but it makes her look sort of unfinished, right? You really need to take care of the whole you. It *all* belongs to God.

All Hands on Deck!
Just Do It

Let's go through a hand-care routine together. You'll probably find all the tools you need around the house, but if not, just skip the step involved and try it later if and when you've had a chance to get what you need.

Tools

- nail polish remover (only if you have nail polish on already) and cotton balls
- large bowl of warm water with some mild soap mixed in
- nail brush or metal nail cleaning thingie (usually found on nail clippers—it's the pointed instrument)
- hand lotion
- cuticle pusher, orange stick, or Q-tip
- manicure scissors
- emery board (nail file)
- if you want to polish—clear base coat, colored polish, clear top coat

Steps

1. Remove all old polish with cotton balls dipped in nail polish remover.
2. File your nails with the emery board. Go in one direction only, toward the center from each side. Zigzagging back and forth weakens your nail. Make sure all your nails are the same length and the same shape. An oval is good.
3. Dip your hands into hot soapy water and let your nails soak for a few minutes. That will make it easier to get dirt out from under your nails with the brush or pointy thing. Rinse well with lukewarm water and dry really well.

4. Put some moisturizing lotion on your hands and let it sink into your skin. Wipe off any from your nails before you go to Step 5.
5. Use the cuticle pusher to gently coax the skin around your nails back off of your nails. If you have a hangnail, use the manicure scissors to gently snip it. Don't tear your skin; it can get easily infected.

If you aren't going to polish, you're done! If you do want to polish, go on to Step 6.

6. Using three strokes to cover your whole nail, put on one layer of base coat. Let it dry completely before you move on. Base coat is important because putting colored polish right on your nails can eventually cause them to look yellow.
7. Put on two layers of the colored polish, again using three strokes and letting it dry between coats.
8. Now put on one layer of top coat or sealer. You guessed it—use three strokes.
9. It takes several hours for your nails to completely dry, so your best bet for keeping them from chipping right away is to do your manicure right before you go to bed. Don't let your nails get water on them until the polish is dry. If you really need to speed up drying time, stand with your hands in the freezer for about two minutes. That will dry the surface, but it will still be a while before all the coats are entirely dry.

Getting to the Bottom of It

Why don't we do the same with your feet? Grab your pedicure equipment:

Tools

- nail polish remover (if your toenails are painted already) and cotton balls
- nail clippers
- a basin of warm water and a towel

- pumice stone
- moisturizer
- orange stick or Q-tip
- if you're going to polish—clear base coat, colored polish, clear top coat

Here we go with the steps (Again, if you don't have the right tool, skip to the next step until you have a chance to get what you need).

Steps

1. Remove any old polish with remover and cotton. Never paint over old polish—yuck!
2. Cut your toenails straight across with the clippers. Don't cut into corners trying to get an oval shape—save that for your fingernails. Cutting away the corners can cause ingrown toenails—very painful!
3. Soak your feet for ten to fifteen minutes in the warm water to soften any calluses you have. It'll feel great—kind of like pampering yourself. Be sure to dry your feet completely—between the toes, too!
4. Use the pumice stone to rub the callused area gently. That gets the dead skin off.
5. With the pointy thing on your nail clippers, clean out any dirt from under your toenails.
6. Massage your feet with moisturizer. If you're going to polish your toenails, be sure to get all the moisturizer off your nails first.
7. Use the orange stick or Q-tip to gently nudge your cuticles back off your nails.

If you aren't going to polish your toenails, you're done!
If you are, read on.

8. Put pieces of cotton between your toes to separate them so your polish won't smudge.
9. Follow the polishing steps for fingernails above (6–9).

Look at you! You're gorgeous right down to your fingertips and toenails!

Toe Troubles and Hand Headaches?

Take off your shoes, socks, and nail polish. Let's look for the common problems you might run into with hands 'n' feet:

1. How often do you wash your hands?

Hopefully you said "a lot," because clean hands are the best protection against germs and bacteria. Always wash after using the bathroom, before you eat, when you've been petting animals, and when you come home from a shopping trip. If you have a cold, double the number of times you wash your hands. If possible, wash every time you blow your nose.

2. Do you bite your nails?

Hopefully if you do bite, it's just your fingernails, not your toenails! But if you are a fingernail nibbler, that's a habit you'll want to break. Not only do nails look pretty nasty when you've chewed them down to the quick, but every time you put your hands in your mouth, you're loading up with germs. Besides, jewelry—no matter how beautiful—doesn't look good on hands with bitten nails. How do you break a longtime habit like that? It isn't easy, but try these tricks:

- Whenever your hands aren't busy, like when you're watching TV, hold onto something little, like a stone, or play with Silly Putty.
- Get some special bad-tasting polish at the drugstore that's made for helping nail biters kick the habit.
- Give yourself a reward when you've gone, say, five days without biting. Keep track on a calendar—and no fair cheating!
- Start giving yourself a weekly manicure, even if you have no nails to speak of. You'll be surprised at how much easier it is to keep filed, polished nails out of your mouth.

3. Do you have warts on your hands or feet?

Not terribly attractive, are they? Keep in mind that they don't look nearly as big to anyone else as they do to you. Besides, they're harmless, just caused by a virus, and usually they'll go away by themselves. The drugstore sells products to help get rid of warts, but they take a month or two to work. A doctor can also remove a wart by freezing it, but the process is a little painful and leaves a scab that takes a while to disappear. Don't pick at warts; that won't help and it may even spread the virus. And don't bother avoiding toads—they don't cause warts, no matter what anyone tells you!

4. Is your nail polish chipped at the moment, or does it get that way a lot?

Nail polish does chip, and as soon as yours starts, take off the polish. Naked nails definitely look better than chipped nails. If you don't have time to do enough manicures to keep up with the chipping, try wearing clear polish. Chips won't show up as much. Remember that it's best not to do a complete manicure more than once a week because nail polish remover can really dry out your nails and make them brittle.

5. Do you have little bubbles in your nail polish?

You probably shook your nail polish too much. Try rolling the bottle between your palms a couple of times instead of shaking it.

6. Are your nails themselves chipped and split, even though you don't bite them?

Your nails are just naturally soft. Bummer. But you can buy a nail hardener that you put on when you do your nails. Even if you do use one, however, don't use your nails for little crowbars or scrapers.

7. Do you have little white spots under your nails?

Not to worry. Those are just bruises that'll grow out.

8. Are your nails so long they get in your way?

If you're blessed with hard nails that grow long and don't break, it can be fun to see how long you can grow them, but that isn't practical, and it doesn't look that wonderful. Somebody once said, "If your pinkie nail is long enough to spear an olive, your nails are too long." Sounds like a good rule of thumb (and every other finger)!

9. Are your feet on the puffy side?

Take the time to put them up for a while every day. It's a great thing to do while reading or talking on the phone. Also, don't sit cross-legged. That slows down the flow of blood to your legs and feet and can cause swollen ankles.

10. Do your feet—well, smell bad?

That can definitely be embarrassing! Once you've got it, nothing but a foot-washing will take it away, so prevention is best. To keep your feet stinkless

- Always wear clean cotton or wool socks; those are natural fibers that absorb sweat, which is what makes your feet give off that delicious aroma in the first place.
- Wear shoes made of natural materials like leather or canvas; those will let your feet breathe, while shoes made out of man-made materials such as plastic are definite stench producers.
- Get the odor out of your shoes by sprinkling baking soda in them and leaving it there overnight. When you shake them out in the morning, they'll be stink-free.
- Try not to wear sneakers all the time; they're the biggest smelly feet culprits.

11. Do your feet just plain hurt?

If you find yourself taking off your shoes every chance you get (in church, at the movies, in restaurants!) you're probably wearing uncomfortable shoes. Always have your feet measured at the shoe store because your feet are still growing. Have both feet measured—some people have two different sizes! (And that doesn't make them freaks.) Walk around in the shoes you're about to buy to be sure they don't rub you the wrong way. Don't buy shoes that are too small, even if the salesperson tells you they'll stretch. They won't! Too big is just as bad.

Check out the heels on your shoes. Flats should have a 3/4" heel—they shouldn't be perfectly flat. High heels are fun on special occasions if you have permission, but don't wear them all day—and don't let them be too high. Really high heels throw your spine out of whack—and besides, they look a little odd on a very short girl! When your heels run down,  have them repaired. That'll help foot comfort, too.

If the soles feel thin, use foam inner soles or foot pads for more cushioning. Otherwise, it's like walking barefoot on a concrete floor. Yikes! Instant foot pain!

Get the tired feeling out of your feet by putting two tablespoons of Epsom salts in two quarts of warm water and resting your feet in there for as long as the water is warm. Then massage gently. Yeah, baby!

12. Do you have blisters on your feet?

Blisters are spots that form where your shoes rub against your skin. Usually they start with a bubble that pops or tears open and leaves a raw place. Don't pop the blister yourself. Put a Band-Aid over it to protect it until it heals, removing it at night so it can get air and heal faster. Then be sure to always wear the right shoes for the right activity. For instance, sneakers are better than dressy flats for long walks.

13. Do you have red, scaly patches between your toes and on the bottoms of your feet?

You probably have a common fungus called *athlete's foot*. They call it that because it grows on warm, moist surfaces like locker room floors, pools, and public showers. To prevent athlete's foot, wear flip-flops or shower shoes when in those places. Dry your feet really well, especially between your toes. Wear shoes that let your feet breathe, and don't wear the same shoes all the time. To get rid of itchy athlete's foot, get yourself an anti-fungal powder, spray, or cream at the drugstore. It's easy to treat.

14. Do you have a painful flat wart on the bottom of either of your feet that hurts especially when you walk barefoot?

That's called a plantar wart which hurts because the weight of your body is pushing it into your skin. A doctor will have to remove it if it really hurts you to walk, but not to worry. The treatments are almost painless.

Talking to God About It

What? You want me to talk to God about my hands and feet?

Sure! Remember, God cares about *all* of you. Think about it in terms of what he made your hands and feet to *do*.

Dear _____*,*

I'm getting a little _____ *by all this talk about manicures and pedicures! Will you help me take care of them so I can be You-Niquely beautiful and healthy? I need that because*_____

_____

The most important things I do with my fingers are (play the piano? eat peanut butter out of the jar?)

_____

_____

The most important things I do with my hands are (show the teacher I know the answers? clap at my brothers' soccer games?)

_____

_____

The most important things I do with my toes are (pick up socks when I'm too lazy to lean over?)

_____

_____

The most important things I do with my feet are (walk to school? dance with my dog?)

_____

_____

God, will you especially help me with _____

_____*? And most of all, will you help me fold my hands in prayer and walk the path you've laid out for me?*

Amen. Amen!

Lily Pad

If you had to give each of your fingers and toes a name, what would they be?

When Beauty Gets Hairy

**Now, son of man, take a sharp sword and
use it as a barber's razor to shave your
head and your beard.**
Ezekiel 5:1

Shave? Me?

At some point, you'll probably start shaving. Now? Well, maybe.

Ever since American women started wearing skirts above the ankle and dresses without sleeves, they've been removing the hair from their legs and armpits to give themselves a cleaner, more ladylike look. Not everybody does it. In Europe, for instance, it isn't unusual to go to a beach and see plenty of leg and pit hair, and nobody seems to be bothered by it.

If you haven't started growing hair under your arms, or the hair below your knees hasn't gotten thicker than it used to be, it will eventually. Then you'll need to decide whether you want to shave or not. If you think you'd like to be hairless in those spots, ask your mom if you can shave.

HOW IS THIS A God Thing?

Like wearing makeup, shaving is one of those things a grown-up needs to approve. Some parents might not want you to grow up too fast, and leg-shaving is a pretty sophisticated thing. Others are leery of turning you loose with a razor! Still others may warn you that once you start, the hair that grows back in will be more stubbly, and then you'll feel like you have to shave. Whatever her reason, if your mom says no, it stands. Ya gotta honor her wisdom for you, because that's why God gave you parents. Besides, she probably won't make you go hairy forever! Try asking her again in another six months.

If She Says Go for It

Shaving's a lot easier than doing pre-algebra or applying eyeliner. Let's walk through it together.

Just Do It

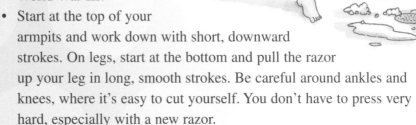

- Shave in the shower or bath because your hair will be at its softest when it's wet.
- Put a bunch of shaving lotion or soap on your armpits or legs.
- Use a clean razor. It's best to have your own—and those disposable ones are so inexpensive. Don't borrow your dad's. That's a good way to start World War III!
- Start at the top of your armpits and work down with short, downward strokes. On legs, start at the bottom and pull the razor up your leg in long, smooth strokes. Be careful around ankles and knees, where it's easy to cut yourself. You don't have to press very hard, especially with a new razor.
- Most girls just shave their legs below their knees. The hair above the knees is usually pretty fine and doesn't need shaving.
- Stop to rinse your razor often so it doesn't get globbed up with hair and soap. Rinse the razor when you're all finished, before putting it away.
- Rinse well. Dry well. Put lotion on your legs and deodorant or an antiperspirant on your armpits. You're good to go.

De-Hairing Hints
Girlz WANT TO KNOW

❀ *LILY: I get these little red bumps when I shave. It looks worse than it did when it was hairy!*

Lily, did you remember to wet the hair before you started? Shaving dry will break you out in a rash faster than poison ivy. Never shave dry—ouch!

❁ *RENI: How often do I have to change these disposable plastic razors, anyway?*

Replace it after you've used it two or three times. That may seem wasteful, but a sharp blade is the secret to a smooth shave. That's why those disposable razors come in packs with lots in them.

❁ *ZOOEY: I tried shaving my legs and I ended up with a bloody mess. My mom said I wasn't trying it again until I'm fourteen!*

You need to listen to your mom. Next time you try shaving, whenever that is, make sure you use a sharp blade. It's a dull blade that causes nicks. Go gently and slowly—don't press hard. And be extra careful in places where bones stick out. Don't worry, you'll get the hang of it.

❁ *SUZIE: I cut myself sometimes, and I can't get it to stop bleeding. Could I bleed to death?*

Probably not. Just rinse off the cut with clear water, dry it up with a tissue, and put a Band-Aid on it. Then read what I told Zooey about preventing bloodletting while shaving!

❁ *KRESHA: My mom won't let me shave my legs and I feel like a gorilla. What can I do?*

First of all, you may *feel* like a gorilla, but I'd be willing to bet you don't *look* like one. Keep in mind that everybody else your age is so busy thinking about their own "stuff," they aren't even looking at your legs, hairy or not. If it makes you feel better about the way you look, wear pants, tights, or long skirts whenever you can. If you are wearing a short skirt or shorts, try not to think about your legs or draw attention to them by trying to hide them! Remember, God-confidence is beautiful no matter what. Even hairy legs can't change that. In a few months, ask your mom again. In the meantime, be as responsible and well-groomed as you can, so that it will seem natural to her that you start shaving your legs. Whining about it won't help that image, believe me!

Talking to God About It

Try a prayer like this when you pray today. You never know where God may take you!

God? This shaving thing is (or isn't) a big deal to me because

_____

_____

_____ .

Maybe I ought to be concentrating on some other things as well. I'm going to close my eyes and lie back and just listen for you for a little while. Will you help me use this quiet time to know what else you want me to be thinking about and doing, in addition to things like shaving my legs? After all, I want to be You-Niquely beautiful, inside and out.

Lily Pad

What's the funkiest spot on your body where you have hair? Write about how funny that is!

chapter
6

Clothesline

*She is clothed in fine linen and purple. . . . She is
clothed with strength and dignity.*
Proverbs 31:22, 25

So You Want to Look Good in Your Clothes ...

The best way to look great is to know your body right now and wear clothes that play up *your* best features and feel good on *you*. Not your sister, your best friend, or the model on the front of *Teen* magazine. You-Nique You.

Girlz WANT TO KNOW

❀ *ZOOEY: How come Ashley and Marcie and Reni can wear those capri pants and look so cute, and then I put them on and everybody laughs?*

Because Ashley's and Marcie's and Reni's bodies are theirs, not yours. Not everybody looks incredible in capris. Of course, people shouldn't laugh at you, and if you *feel* good in capri pants, you could just ignore the teasers, remembering that *they* are the fools. But it might be easier for you, and a lot more fun, to decide what kind of pants *do* look good on you and wear those. Get a grown-up to go to a store with you and get a pile of different styles of pants and try them all on. Which ones make you smile at yourself in the mirror? Which ones can you really move around in the way you like to? Those are the ones to wear. And wear them proudly. You are You-Niquely beautiful.

❀ *KRESHA: I have little bitty shoulders and ENORMOUS hips! No clothes look good on me. I always look like a walking pear!*

You probably don't actually look like a "walking pear" or any other fruit. Remember what we said about our pictures of our own bodies? But if you want things to look more balanced, then wear white or light colors on top. Full blouses or ones with pockets will even things out. The opposite goes

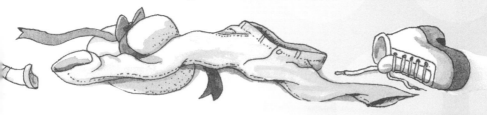

for girls with nice broad shoulders and slim hips. They can get a balance by wearing loose pants or skirts with simple, streamlined blouses and tops. Pretty tricky, huh?

❁ *LILY: I'm so tall! I'm trying to accept me just the way God made me. But, sometimes my clothes look kinda silly.*

Don't wear anything short, Lily, like really short skirts or rib-tickling tops. Of course, don't wear big ol' heels, either. Then straighten your shoulders, hold your head high, and love being stately.

❁ *RENI: I have the opposite problem. I'm way short, and some of my clothes make me look even more like a shrimp.*

Nothing wrong with being short. You're petite. Dainty. Pleasantly elfish. If you'd like to feel a little taller, just for fun, wear the same color clothes from your hat to your shoes. It'll look like you've added inches.

Check Yourself OUT

Let's get in front of that mirror again and have some fun with finding out more about your You-Nique You. Look at yourself (you're getting to like you now, aren't you?) and answer these questions. Then see what the answers tell you.

What are your three very best features? Do you have curly hair, sparkly eyes, and great legs? Or is your trio your big smile, broad shoulders, and tiny waist? Write yours here.

1.
2.
3.

Clothes Tip: Use "attention-catchers" like these on or near those features:

- Warm colors like reds, oranges, and yellows—light and bright
- Big patterns and bold textures like large plaids or rough tweeds
- Shiny fabrics like satin

- Glitter, sequins, or rhinestones
- Fancy details like ruffles, lace, or embroidery
- Jewelry and scarves

For example, on that tiny waist, wear fun belts. On that curly hair? Go for bright-colored scrunchies or shiny barrettes.

Get the idea?

What are the three features you aren't as happy with (remembering that God loves 'em all)**?** Are you self-conscious about your nose? Do you feel as if your long arms are everywhere? Do you wish your calves were more slender? Write your three here, but be KIND to yourself in the way you describe them!

1.
2.
3.

Clothes Tip: Don't use the attention-catchers on or near any feature you want to play down.

For example, bright red tights aren't the best choice if you don't want eyes drawn to your calves. A ball cap that points right to your nose won't draw attention *away* from it.

Which of these best describes the things you like to do? You might be a combination of some of these, so if that's the case, number them 1, 2, and 3, with 1 being the one you are most of the time.

_____ A. Anything that involves sports or just being active, like softball, swimming, riding my bike. I hate to sit around!

_____ B. Anything that makes me think, like reading, writing, playing board games, doing stuff at the computer, or even watching really good movies. As long as I'm using my mind, I'm happy.

_____ C. Anything that makes me either laugh or cry, like reading, writing, watching movies, playing pretend games, daydreaming, being in plays. Let me feel emotions and I'm good to go!

Clothes Tip: Not only is it more fun to wear clothes that make you look your best, but it's a blast to wear things that match your *style*. We can change styles as often as we want—it's fun to experiment. But when it comes to really feeling like *you*, you might want to think about wearing clothes that tell who you are.

If you answered A, the sporty style might suit you best. Don't fill up your closet with too many frills, because you're probably most comfortable in things you can really move around in. That might mean jeans and T-shirts or fun sneakers in every color or even those cool dresses made out of T-shirt material.

If you answered B, think about the tailored look. That doesn't mean boring! It could mean khakis instead of jeans. Maybe for you it's great sweaters and pleated plaid skirts. You're just the type who can pull off a pair of saddle Oxfords!

If you answered C, chances are you like anything romantic. Wear ruffles and lace if you want—and even if nobody else is doing it. Grab that embroidered vest your sister is about to give to Goodwill. Put on pink socks with your tennis shoes. You're a dreamer, so dream up outfits that are completely you.

Just Do it

You don't need a lot of clothes to get the look you want. You can probably get it with the stuff you already have. Take an afternoon when you can pull everything out of your closet and put it on your bed. As you put each item back into your closet, play around with it, and ask yourself these questions:

- How many other things does it go with? You can wear those red overalls with white, blue, and red prints of course, but what about yellow? Or green? A piece of jewelry or a hair gizzie that has those same two colors will tie it together and you've got a smashing outfit that is totally you!
- If it doesn't shout your style all by itself, what can you do with it to get it there? Did you ever think of wearing that silky skirt you think is too fussy with your denim vest? You can be sporty AND dressed up.
- Does it really not fit you right? Or do you just know that no matter what you do with it, it still isn't going to be you? Put everything like that into a box to give to a worthy cause. It's bound to be *somebody's* fit and style.

What Would God Think of Your Clothes?

He cares about my *clothes?*

HOW IS THIS A God Thing?

Your clothes tell as much about you as anything you tell people about yourself. If you're into the grunge thing, that tells people you really don't care how you look and that basically everything is a downer—even if that's not how you really feel. If you run around in short shorts and itty-bitty tops, you scream, *"I'm a boy-chaser!"* without even opening your mouth.

What *does* God want us to say with our clothes? He spells it out for us in the Bible. (Isn't that just like him?)

Just in case you were thinking about forgetting the whole clothes thing all together and joining a nudist colony, God does want us to wear clothes. He made the very first ones for Adam and Eve.

> **The LORD God made garments of skin for Adam and his wife and clothed them.**
> *(Gen. 3:21)*

He wants your clothes to say you're a girl. I don't think he means we women can't put on a ball cap and sweatshirt, but we do need to show the world that we are You-Niquely feminine.

A woman must not wear men's clothing, nor a man wear women's clothing, for the LORD your God detests anyone who does this.
(Deut. 22:5)

He wants your clothes to say you're a woman who worships him. That means he wants you to dress modestly—not "strutting your stuff"!

I also want women to dress modestly, with decency and propriety, not with braided hair or gold or pearls or expensive clothes, but with good deeds, appropriate for women who profess to worship God.
(1 Tim. 2:9–10)

He wants your clothes to say you don't need the most expensive, the flashiest, the most bizarre, or the one with the most popular label. He wants them to let your true beauty come from the inside.

Your beauty should not come from outward adornment.... Instead, it should be that of your inner self, the unfading beauty of a gentle and quiet spirit, which is of great worth in God's sight.
(1 Peter 3:3–4)

He wants them to say, "I respect myself and my God." That means looking the very best you can, because you're happy to be you.

**She is clothed with strength and dignity;
she can laugh at the days to come.**
(Prov. 31:25)

But EVERYBODY Has One!

Sometimes it feels like there's nothing worse than not having the most hip thing that everybody else has. It makes you feel like a loser, right? Like you're totally out of it. Like the biggest geek since . . .

Well, you get the idea. And believe it or not, so does your mom. Girls have been begging their moms for what's hot as far back as history goes. Girls in the 1920s wanted short skirts (in the '20s, that meant above the ankle!) and bobbed hair, and they whined to be allowed to wear their galoshes unbuckled because everybody else was doing it. Girls in the 1960s hankered for love beads and tie-dyed stuff. Girls in the 1980's wanted three pairs of socks to match each outfit, and wore them all at the same time! Look at some photographs of your mom when she was your age. Can you stand it! No telling what *your* daughter is going to try to get you to buy for her!

It's natural to want to fit in. There isn't even anything wrong with it— unless doing it is going to mess up something else that's much more impor- tant. Try following these guidelines when you're shopping for clothes with the grown-up in your life.

Things You Should Avoid Whining for While Shopping

1. Anything you know your family can't afford. If you see your mom scrambling in the bottom of her purse for change in the grocery store, don't ask for the tennis shoes with all the bells and whistles on them.
2. Anything your mom or dad has already said no to. If you handle their decision in a mature way, the answer might be yes the next time you ask for something.
3. Anything you know is bad news, no matter how cool everybody else thinks it is. Maybe anybody that's anybody is wearing a necklace with a skull on it, but why even bring it up when you know it's all about death?
4. Anything trendy if you have a whole closet full of trendy stuff that went out of style in a week and hasn't been worn since.

But I Wanna Be Cool!

• So start your own trends. Get all your Christian friends to wear crosses all the time. Do cool things with your church camp T-shirts. Bring wearing skirts back in style!

- Be so You-Niquely You that no one cares whether you have Tommy Hilfiger or K-Mart. If you look around, you'll discover that the really cool people are the ones other people like because of who they are, not what they wear.
- If money's the only problem, work around the house and for neighbors to earn the cash to buy that trendy fad thing you want. Chances are, when you get to the checkout counter and have to part with your hard-earned money, you'll think hard about whether that "cool" thing is really worth it!

Talking to God About It

Dear _____,

We talked about a lot of stuff in this chapter. Will you help me sort it out?

Will you help me figure out who I really am so I can reflect that in the things I wear?

_____

Will you help me accept my body and be happy looking my best instead of trying to look someone else's best?

_____

Will you help me make the most of everything I have?

_____

Will you help me to show that I love and respect myself and you even in the things I wear?

_____

Will you help me to be accepted for who I am, instead of for how many of the latest clothes I wear?

_____

Thanks, God. I knew I could count on you.
Love,

_____

Lily Pad

Describe your dream outfit—the perfect ensemble that would show you exactly as you are, fit perfectly, show off all your best features, and be fun to wear. Describe it in detail, head to toe. Make it an outfit God would love!

Describe your deam outfit. . . . Make it an outfit God would love!

Don't Trash Your Temple!

Do you not know that your body is a temple of the Holy Spirit, who is in you, whom you have received from God? ... Therefore honor God with your body.

1 Corinthians 6:19–20

HOW IS THIS A God Thing?

Because your BODY is a God thing! Not only did God create it, but it's now filled with the Holy Spirit. Doing anything but taking care of it and respecting it and using it for God is like dumping a load of garbage in the middle of the sanctuary!

Usually when we talk about taking care of our temple-bodies, we're thinking about healthy food and exercise and not smoking or using illegal drugs. But "trashing your temple" on the outside is just as upsetting to God as messing it up on the inside. Some of the things that are considered cool right now are the same as painting graffiti on the front of the temple—*your* temple.

Girlz WANT TO KNOW About Body Piercing

✿ *ZOOEY: My mom won't let me get my ears pierced. She says I'll look like some kind of hussy or something—and besides, she says knowing me, they'll probably get infected.*

Once again, you need to honor your mom by doing—and not doing!—as she asks. Her ideas about jewelry may come from I Timothy 2:9, where it says women shouldn't deck themselves out with gold and pearls instead of with good deeds. You might think that means something a little different, but for now, what Mom says goes. As for infections, they sometimes do happen with ear-piercings. If and when the time comes, go to a place with a reputation for doing good clean work (don't let a friend do it with an ice cube and a sewing needle!). Then keep your new holes clean with hydrogen peroxide or the solution the store will give you. Keep your earrings clean, too. Until Mom says

yes, show her how capable you are of taking care of the rest of your body. She might change her mind sooner than you think.

🌸 *LILY: My parents let me get my ears pierced, but they said a flat-out NO to having it done to my tongue, nose, or belly button. What's the difference?*

For one thing, although ear piercing has become common, putting holes in other parts of your body to put jewelry in them still carries the look and feel of someone really trying to draw attention to herself. Girls with pierced noses and tongues tend to *look* rebellious and disrespectful, even if they aren't. They sometimes set themselves up for unnecessary battles that way.

For another, ear piercing doesn't really interfere with other bodily functions. Your earlobes just kind of hang there. But your nose and your tongue have jobs to do, and a gold post or ring stuck in there gets in the way.

Besides all that, we've been talking about the whole beautiful you. A big ol' rhinestone in your eyebrow doesn't say "Look at the You-Niquely Beautiful me," it says, "Look at my eyebrow!" Now, what's up with that?

Girlz WANT TO KNOW About Tattoos

🌸 *RENI: I heard that getting a tattoo really hurts. Is that true?*

They do it with a needle, injecting permanent dye into your skin. Does that tell you anything?

🌸 *SUZIE: I heard getting a tattoo could be dangerous. Is it?*

You heard right. Anytime anyone injects a needle into your skin, there's a danger of passing germs and bacteria into your body. We're not talking about just getting a rash here. A person can get hepatitis, even AIDS, from a contaminated needle. That doesn't mean it always happens. Many tattoo artists use sterile procedures. But why chance it for a picture in your skin?

❀ *LILY: You can't get rid of a tattoo, can you?*

It's tough. It requires another procedure most people don't want to go through. Why do it in the first place?

❀ *KRESHA: Would it be all right to get the kind you just stick on?*

Is it all right with—you guessed it—your parents? They might not like even the *idea* of a tattoo, real or fake. Leviticus 19:28 does say, "Do not . . . put tattoo marks on yourselves." Of course, Leviticus 19:27 also says, "Do not . . . clip off the edges of your beard." Just check it out with your folks before you start sticking things on!

Sometimes I Just Want to Be Different!

Have you ever gone into a beauty shop and looked at some of the hair-style books? Aren't those 'dos bizarre sometimes? Hair sticking straight up or straight out or all pointing toward the front like a bunch of arrows!

And have you ever thought, "I'd like to do that, just go to extremes"?

It would be safer with clothes, of course, because you can always change them. You're sort of stuck with a hairstyle . . .

Before you go any further with that daydream, let's talk to God about it.

Talking to God About It

Pray this little prayer:

Dear God,
I love you. I want to be exactly who you want me to be. I want to
be You-Niquely beautiful, but I don't want to distract anybody from

seeing you in me. When people look at me, I want them to be reminded of how good you are, what a great job you did making me. I want the way I look on the outside to be a God thing. Thanks for making me.
    Amen.

Now think about going to extremes again.
Amen!

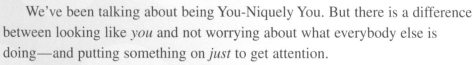

CHECK Yourself OUT

We've been talking about being You-Niquely You. But there is a difference between looking like *you* and not worrying about what everybody else is doing—and putting something on *just* to get attention.

Shall we check that out? Read each of these stories. If any one reminds you of something you've done or are doing now, put a check mark next to it. Then give it some serious thought and prayer. Talk to your parents about it. Are you going a little extreme, or is that just an expression of that very special You?

- -

Keely decided it was going to be her trademark to always have a teddy bear sticking out of her clothes someplace. The bear's head would be peeking out between the buttons on her flannel shirt or poking from the waistband of her jeans. People started referring to her as "The Teddy Bear Girl."

- -

Jessie really wanted to have her head shaved so she could feel like her body was her own. She nagged about it so much her parents finally said, "Go for it." At first it was cool having people she didn't even know come up to her and ask her why she did it so she could say, "Because I wanted to." Then that got old and she wished everybody would just deal with it.

- -

Emmy got bored in school a lot and would draw on herself with felt tip markers. When everybody told her how neat that was, she started doing it all the time. There was a heart on one cheek, a star on the other, and sometimes whole scenes on her arms and legs!

- -

Christie wanted to start a trend, so she began wearing only pink. She was rosy from scrunchie to tennies. It caught on with some of her friends, until they looked like a bottle of Pepto-Bismol when they were together. Others chose their own colors and wore just purple or totally yellow. Still others started a rumor that Christie was the leader of some weird cult.

Lily Pad

If I wanted to show the very most unique part of me, in a God-thing way, using my appearance, I would . . .

What If I Have to Put Up with . . . ?

He had no beauty or majesty to attract us to him, nothing in his appearance that we should desire him.

Isaiah 53:2

Glasses? Braces? Becoming Amazon woman? I don't want to look like a weirdo!

Of course you don't. No one does. But there isn't an appearance "flaw" that can't be overcome—if not turned into the best part of you!

HOW IS THIS A God Thing?

Go back to that mirror we've been using. Take another long look at your friend in there (You-Nique You!) and focus on that physical thing you're struggling with—those glasses or those braces or that birthmark.

Now read below what God has to say about it. Every time you see a blank, write your "hang-up" in there.

A person with _____ "may eat the most holy food of God."
(Leviticus 21:22)

So in the first place, when it comes to whether he loves you or not, God couldn't care less whether you wear glasses or have braces or sport the biggest wart in life. "Come on in," he says!

Praise be to the God of all comfort, who comforts us in our

_____.
(2 Corinthians 1:4)

Grown-ups may tell you glasses or braces or funky moles are no big deal, but God understands how hard that is right now. Go to him—he's there with the comfort.

Neither _____ nor _____ will be able to separate us from the love of God that is in Christ Jesus our Lord.
(Romans 8:39)

So do they really matter *so* much when you get right down to it?

People look at the _____, but the Lord looks at the heart.
(1 Samuel 16:7)

So concentrate on who you are inside. Sure, other people may still stare at your 10,000 freckles or tease you about being tall, but working on your spiritual self will make you less self-conscious. And eventually, people will even start to comment, "You're getting to be so pretty." Most of them won't even know why!

Look at your friend in the mirror again—the one who knows she's loved, the one who realizes those knobby knees don't mean squat to the beautiful person. Ya gotta love her, don't ya?

Now, do her a favor and let that "flaw" become an asset. Read on!

Girlz WANT TO KNOW About Glasses

❀ *ZOOEY: I think I might need glasses, but I don't know if I want to wear them. Won't they make me look ugly?*

First of all, your eyesight comes first. If you have any of these symptoms, ask your parents to have your eyes examined by an optometrist. You may need glasses if

- you get headaches from reading;
- you have to squint your eyes to see things, either up close or far away;
- you sometimes have double vision.

And, no, they don't necessarily have to make you look ugly! The optometrist or eye center where you go will have a selection of frames and a wall full of mirrors. Experiment with as many colors, shapes, and sizes as you want until you find something that makes you smile at yourself. They say there's a hat to suit everyone; I'm sure that's true of glasses, too.

❁ *SUZIE: I have to wear glasses when I read, and I feel ridiculous! I'm just about the only one in the class who has them on.*

Lots of people's eyes start to change around your age and on into the teens. Pretty soon, as you look around, you'll see more and more people whipping them out to see the board or read the textbook. Right now, you're unique, so pick out the cutest pair you can find and be as adorable as you are!

❁ *LILY: My mom makes me wear sunglasses on bright days, but they make me look like a mosquito or something!*

Your mom's right. Sunglasses will protect your eyes from ultraviolet rays. Maybe you've chosen the wrong style. Your best bet for sunglasses or regular specs are frames that don't extend past the sides of your face. Right now, small glasses that just cover your eyes are popular. Try a pair of those and see if they aren't fun. The right sunglasses can give you a mysterious, classy air!

❁ *RENI: If I had to have glasses, I'd get me some contact lenses.*

Contacts definitely help you see better without changing the way you look, but they require care and cleaning, and they can be tough to get used to at first.

Girlz WANT TO KNOW About Braces

❁ *RENI: I just found out I have to have braces. I can hear the boys at school now calling me "Tinsel Teeth" and "Metal Mouth."*

78

Remember what to do about teasing: ignore and pray. And besides, braces aren't so bad anymore. They come in colors, and so do the rubber bands you might have to use. We're talking everything from baby blue to neon. Get some cool ones, and then smile, smile, smile! You'll dazzle the daylights out of those teasers.

🌸 *KRESHA: People with braces usually look all yellow-toothed and stuff. I don't want that!*

It doesn't have to be that way if you take care of them. Brush after every meal or snack. (You might start a trend in the bathroom at school. Get yourself a neat toothbrush and a miniature tube of toothpaste and keep them in a cool zippered bag in your backpack.) At least once a day, really go for it with the cleaning, maybe with a Water Pic or some dental floss. Not only will you keep your smile shiny now, but you'll avoid gunky-looking teeth when the braces come off. Avoid foods that will stick to your teeth and practically have to be pried off with a crowbar—like caramel apples and Gummy Bears.

What If I'm Too Tall?

Or too short? What if I'm way behind the other girls physically? Or, sometimes worse, way ahead?

We've talked before about NOT comparing yourself to other people, but it's hardest when the other girls are showing off their new bras at a sleepover, or when no boy wants to be paired up with you in folk dancing because he doesn't want to look in your belly button. We need a little more reassurance from God on that.

Talking to God About It

The first thing you need to do is vent to God. He knows what's on your mind, but just like your parents, he likes to hear you say it. Write your gripe (or your multiple complaints) on these lines, the way you'd like to say them to the Big Dad.

*God, I know you knew best when you made me, but could we talk about my*_____.

It really bothers me because _____

_____.

Thanks for listening. Amen.

Now *you* try listening. Find a quiet place (that's tough in some houses!), sit back, close your eyes. Just be with God for a few minutes. Try to chase all other thoughts out of your head except the ones about him. Relax. Think God. Breathe God in. Enjoy a little P&Q (peace and quiet)with the Guy who made you.

Try that every day for several days—praying and then getting quiet. In the meantime, during the rest of your day, be alert for God's answers in things other people say, in things you read in your Bible, in new thoughts that come into your head. Girls who've tried it report that God has told them

- "It's a process. You didn't pop out in the delivery room with all your teeth and hair, right? Give me time to let you grow into yourself."
- "It isn't always going to be like this. Boys will grow taller. Other girls will grow bigger chests and catch up. You might feel like a sore thumb now, but give me time. I have a separate growing plan for each of you."
- "It's a big deal now because it's all new. But very soon you're going to stop caring so much about whether you're the most flat-chested girl in the class. You can hurry that along by concentrating on other things—like *me*!"
- "I happen to like you exactly the way you are this minute. Because you hate it when other people tease you about being short, you hardly ever tease anyone else. In fact, you give people compliments whenever you get the chance. Would you be like that if I hadn't made you the class shorty?"

When you discover what God's saying to you—and you will if you pay attention—write it here. You might want to look back at it now and then!

God said: _____
_____

Just Do It

Lily has written down her BIG UGLINESS, as she calls it. Then she's prayed, like you did above, and she's come up with five things she's going to do to make her "flaw" a cool thing to have. Look back through this chapter and see if you can't do the same for yours.

Lily Robbins

My BIG UGLY is my height. I am like the Empire State Building in a classroom full of Fisher Price play-houses. I am so serious!

But I've prayed and I've read my Bible and I've read this book, and I think there are things I can do about it.

1. I am so not going to pay any attention to Shad Shifferdecker when he teases me. He can call me Robbins Tower all he wants, but I'm just going to ignore him. When it hurts my feelings, I'm going to vent to God—and pray that Shad will actually grow up someday!
2. I made a list of all the good things about being tall—like I can always reach stuff, I can always see over the crowd, people think I'm older than I am and don't treat me like a little kid—that kind of thing. I keep it in my binder so when I start to feel like Andre the Giant, I look at it and sometimes it helps.
3. I keep remembering God made me and so he must like me this way. It would be kind of rude to try to be different, so I'm concentrating on my posture, standing up really straight and tall and all that.
4. My dad told me that when I grow into myself, I'm going to be stat-uesque. I don't know exactly what that means, but I like the sound of it. Sometimes, if I have to walk up to the front of the room or something, I say to myself over and over, "I'm statuesque, I'm statuesque."

Now you try it!

My "big ugliness": _____

Things I think God wants me to do about that: (You don't have to be as long-winded as Lily!)

_____

Lily Pad

When I have my own daughters I'm going to show them pictures of me at this age and tell them how funny it was dealing with my_____.

Here's how I'm gonna tell it...

You Go, Girl!

**Your beauty should come from your inner self,
the unfading beauty of a gentle and quiet spirit,
which is of great worth in God's sight.**

1 Peter 3:4

Remember God-Confidence?

That's what this whole book has been about, isn't it? Learning that you are a gorgeous girl because God loved you enough to make you exactly the way he wanted you to be. Knowing that gives you God-confidence, and there isn't a woman alive with that who doesn't turn every head when she walks into a room. People may not know *why* you're beautiful. They may mutter to each other, "She isn't the typical pretty, but there's something about her . . ."

Let's not leave our look at the You-Niquely Beautiful You without making sure you're on your way to having that "unfading beauty of a gentle and quiet spirit" that gives you God-confidence. (And don't let the gentle-quiet part scare you. Even we motormouths can have it!)

✓ CHECK Yourself OUT

First, find out that you're already on your way. Circle the very best honest answer to each of the questions on the following page.

Have you given up dissing the way you look?
> **Yeah, baby!**
> **Getting there.**
> **Uh, not yet . . .**

Are you now laughing at how ridiculously unreal most advertising is?
> **Yeah, baby!**
> **Getting there.**
> **Uh, not yet . . .**

Have you stopped playing the Comparison Game?
> **Yeah, baby!**
> **Getting there.**
> **Uh, not yet . . .**

Have you learned how to deal with teasing?
> **Yeah, baby!**
> **Getting there.**
> **Uh, not yet . . .**

Do you know what is You-Niquely beautiful about you?

Yeah, baby!

Getting there.

Uh, not yet . . .

Are you taking good care of your hair? Keeping it healthy and styled just for you?

Yeah, baby!

Getting there.

Uh, not yet . . .

Are you taking good care of your skin because it's an important part of your temple?

Yeah, baby!

Getting there.

Uh, not yet . . .

Are you following your parents' decisions regarding your looks?

Yeah, baby!

Getting there.

Uh, not yet . . .

Are you paying attention to your hands 'n' feet, too, because you respect yourself enough to take care of every detail?

Yeah, baby!

Getting there.

Uh, not yet . . .

Are you wearing clothes God would love?

Yeah, baby!

Getting there.

Uh, not yet . . .

Are you avoiding trashing your temple on the outside?

Yeah, baby!

Getting there.

Uh, not yet . . .

Are you turning your biggest "flaw" into one of the best parts of you?

Yeah, baby!

Getting there.

Uh, not yet . . .

Are you learning how to talk to God about *everything?*

Yeah, baby!

Getting there.

Uh, not yet . . .

Are you convinced that you're beautiful?

Yeah, baby!

Getting there.

Uh, not yet . . .

Now look back at your answers.

The **Yeah, baby!** answers tell you that you're really making progress in those areas. Keep it up. The more you do them, the more beautiful you're going to feel—and be.

The **Getting there** answers show where you're working and need to keep on working to get rid of junk-attitudes so there's room for the truth. I'm proud of you. Go, girl!

The **Uh, not yet** . . . answers are pretty important. They tell you what to focus on. What to pray about. What to ask your mom or some other friend you really trust to help you with. Notice they aren't final **No's.** We are all God's works in progress. The job isn't done. At least you know what needs to happen. With God's help, you'll get there.

Final Words Ya Gotta Love

As you're working on all the outside things we've talked about in this book, keep reminding yourself that your God-confidence is what makes you more truly beautiful than a weekly manicure and the most expensive hair conditioner. It's the quiet, gentle spirit that makes people wonder what your secret is.

But you can't just get up tomorrow morning and say, "From now on, I'm going to have a quiet, gentle spirit." Like skin care and hair care and clothes care, you have to do spirit care, too. And like all those other beauty regimens, it takes time and certain beautiful-spirit disciplines.

Here are a few that are guaranteed to get you nearer and nearer to the God who shapes your spirit:

- Having a quiet time with God every day, praying and listening at least twenty minutes.
- Reading God's Word and thinking about how it applies to you, right that very moment. You can make it part of your quiet time.
- Journaling, like you've started to do on your Lily Pads.
- Surrounding yourself with other beautiful Christians as your very best friends.
- Treating those friends—and everyone—the way you've learned to treat yourself.

Oh, and there's one last one. It's the very simplest thing in this book, and yet it's the one guaranteed to make you more beautiful than just about anything else you can do. Ready for it?

Smile.

It won't be hard. After all, God loves you.

And ya gotta love that.

1
Lily
SERIES

Here's Lily!

Nancy Rue

If you liked *The Beauty Book*, you'll love its fictional companion book *Here's Lily!*

Chapter 1

"Leo, don't let it touch you, man! It'll burn your skin off!"

Shad Shifferdecker grabbed his friend's arm and yanked him away from the water fountain just as Lily Robbins leaned over to take a drink. Leo barely missed being brushed by Lily's flaming red hair.

Lily straightened up and drove her vivid blue eyes into Shad.

"I need for you to quit making fun of my hair," she said through her gritted teeth. She always gritted her teeth when she talked to Shad Shifferdecker.

"Why can't you ever just say 'shut up'?" Shad asked. "Why do you always have to sound like a counselor or something?"

Lily didn't know what a counselor sounded like. She'd never been to one. If Shad had, it hadn't helped much as far as she was concerned. He was still rude.

"I'm just being polite," Lily answered.

Leo blinked his enormous gray eyes at Shad. "Shad, can you say 'polite'?"

"Shut up," Shad said and gave Leo a shove that landed him up against Daniel Tibbetts, his other partner in seeing how hateful a sixth-grade boy can be to a sixth-grade girl.

Just then Ms. Gooch appeared at the head of the line, next to the water fountain, and held up her right hand. Hands shot up down the line as mouths closed and most everybody craned their necks to see her. Ms. Gooch was almost shorter than Lily.

"All right, people." Lily was glad she didn't call them "boys and girls" the way the librarian did. "We're going to split up now. Boys will come with me—girls will go into the library."

"How come?" Shad blurted out, as usual.

"The girls are going to a grooming workshop," Ms. Gooch said. She raised an eyebrow—because Ms. Gooch could say more with one black eyebrow than most people could with a whole sentence. "Did you want to go with the girls and learn how to fix your hair and have great skin, Shad? I'm sure they'd love to have you."

No, we would not, Lily wanted to say. But she never blurted out. She just turned to Reni and rolled her eyes.

Reni rolled hers back. That was the thing about best friends, Lily had decided a while back. You could have entire conversations with each other, just by rolling your eyes or saying one key word that sent you both into giggle spasms.

"No way!" Shad bellowed. "I don't want to look like no girl!"

"*Any* girl," Ms. Gooch said. "All right, ladies—go on to the library. Come back with beauty secrets!"

Lily took off on Reni's heels in the direction of the library. Behind her, she heard Shad say—just loudly enough for her to hear—"That grooming lady better be pretty good if she's gonna do anything with Lily!"

"Yeah, dude!" Leo echoed.

Daniel just snorted.

"Ignore them," Reni whispered to Lily as they pushed through the double doors to the inside of the school. "My mama says when boys say things like that, it means they like you."

"Gross!" Lily wrinkled her nose.

Besides, that was easy for Reni to say. Lily thought Reni was about the cutest girl in the whole sixth grade. She was black (Ms. Gooch said they were supposed to call her "African-American," but Reni said that took too long to say) and her skin was the smooth, rich color of Lily's dad's coffee when he put a couple of drops of milk in it. *Mine's more like the milk, without the coffee!* Lily thought.

And even though Reni's hair was a hundred times curlier than Lily's naturally frizzy mass of auburn, it was always in little pigtails or braids or something. Her hair was under control, anyway. Lily's brother Art said Lily's hair always looked like enough for thirty-seven people the way it stuck out all over her head.

But most important of all, Reni was as petite as a toy poodle, not tall and leggy like a giraffe. At least, that was the way Lily thought of herself. Even now, as they walked into the library, Lily tripped on the wipe-your-feet mat and plowed into a rolling rack of books. She rolled with it right into Mrs. Blain, the librarian, who said, "Boys and girls, please be careful where you're walking."

It's just girls, Lily wanted to say to her. *And I'm so glad.* Wouldn't Shad Shifferdecker have had something to say about *that* little move?

Reni steered her to a seat in the front row of the half circles of chairs that had been formed in the middle of the library. The chairs faced a woman who busily took brushes and combs and tubes of things out of a classy-looking leather bag and set them on a table. Lily watched her for a minute.

The lady wore her blond hair short and combed-with-her-fingers, the way all the women did on TV; her nails were long and polished red, and they clacked against the table when she set things down on

7

it. Lily could smell her from the front row—she smelled expensive, like a department store cosmetics counter.

Lily thought about how her mother grabbed lipstick while they were shopping for groceries at Acme and then only put it on when Dad dragged her to some university faculty party. As for having her nails done—high school P.E. teachers didn't *have* fingernails.

Lily's mind and eyes wandered off to the bookshelves. *I'd much rather be finding a book on Indian headdresses,* she thought as she looked wistfully at the plastic book covers shining under the lights. Her class was doing reports on Native Americans, and she had a whole bunch of feathers at home that she'd collected from their family's camping trips. Wouldn't it be cool to make an actual headdress—

"May I have your attention please, ladies?"

Reluctantly Lily peeled her eyes off the Indian books and looked at the lady with the long fingernails. She was facing them now, and Lily saw that she had matching lipstick, put on without a smudge, and dainty gold earrings that danced playfully against her cheek. Something about her made Lily tuck her own well-bitten nails under her thighs and wish she'd looked in the mirror before she came in here to make sure she didn't have playground dirt smeared across her forehead.

Nah, she thought. *If I did, Shad Shifferdecker would've said something about it.*

Besides, the lady had a sparkle in her eyes that made it seem like she could take on Shad Shifferdecker. Lily liked that.

"I'm Kathleen Winfrey," the lady was saying, "and I'm here from the Rutledge Modeling Agency here in Burlington."

An excited murmur went through the girls, followed by a bunch of hands shooting up.

"Well!" Kathleen Winfrey smiled, revealing a row of very white, perfect teeth. Lily sucked in her full lips and hoped her mouth didn't look quite so big.

"Questions already?" Kathleen said. "I've barely started. How about you?"

She pointed to Marcie McCleary who was waving her arm so hard, Lily knew all her rings were going to go flying across the library any second.

"You're from a modeling agency?" Marcie asked breathlessly. "Do you—like—hire models?"

"We hire them, and we train them," Kathleen answered.

"Could we be models?" somebody else asked.

"Is that why you're here—to pick models?"

"Do they do—like—commercials or just fashion shows and stuff?"

"I was at this fashion show at the mall—and this lady came up to my mother and said I could be a model like the ones they had there and—"

"Ladies!" Kathleen interrupted. She laughed in a light, airy kind of way. "Why don't I tell you why I *am* here, and that will probably answer *all* your questions at once. I've come to Cedar Hills Elementary today to talk to you about taking good care of your hair and skin and nails, not to hire models."

The whole library seemed to give a disappointed sigh. Except Lily. It had never occurred to her to be a model in the first place, so what was there to be bummed out about? As for learning how to take good care of her hair and skin and nails—

Lily pulled out her hands and scowled at the nails bitten down to quicks. *I need all the help I can get,* she thought. That evil Shad Shifferdecker was probably right: this lady *better* be pretty good!

"Not everyone is model material," Kathleen went on. "Just as everyone is not doctor material or astronaut material—"

"Or boy material." That came from Ashley Adamson, *the* most boy-crazy girl in the entire *school*. Lily turned to Reni to roll her eyes just in time to see Ashley pointing right at her and whispering to

Chelsea, her fellow boy-chaser. Lily could feel her face stinging as if Ashley had hauled off and slapped her.

"But every woman can be beautiful," Kathleen said. "And since you are all on the edge of young womanhood right now, I'd like to show you some ways that you can discover your own beauty."

This time Lily looked straight ahead so she couldn't see what Ashley was doing. As it was, she heard Ashley sniff, as if she'd discovered her beauty long ago and could show *Kathleen* a thing or two.

"Now," Kathleen said, "I'm going to take you through some basics in skin care, hair care, nail care—but instead of just telling you, I'd like to show you. I'm going to pick someone—"

She took a step forward, and a sea of hands sprang up and waved like seaweed in a lake. Marcie held onto her arm with the other hand as if she were afraid it would pop off, and Ashley's face went absolutely purple as she strained for Kathleen to see her. Even Reni raised her hand tentatively, although she rolled her eyes at Lily as if to say, *She'll never pick me, so why am I bothering?*

Lily seemed to be the only one who wasn't begging Kathleen to look at her. If she did, she knew she'd have Ashley and Chelsea and some of the others hooting and pointing and whispering. *Lily—you? Too tall Lily? With too much red hair? Too big a mouth and too thick lips? What are you thinking?*

Instead, Lily reached over, grabbed Reni's arm, and held it up even higher. It was at exactly that moment that Kathleen's eyes stopped scanning the desperate little crowd and rested on her.

"Ah—you," she crooned.

"Yay!" Lily squeezed Reni's hand. "She picked you, Reni!"

But Kathleen shook her head and smiled. "No, honey," she said to Lily. "I picked *you*."

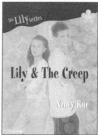 
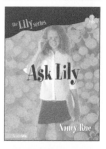 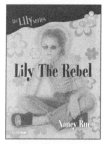
 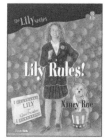

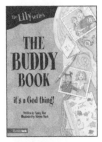

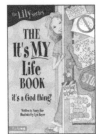

NIV Young Women of Faith Bible
GENERAL EDITOR SUSIE SHELLENBERGER

Designed just for girls ages 8-12, the *NIV Young Women of Faith Bible* not only has a trendy, cool look, it's packed with fun to read in-text features that spark interest, provide insight, highlight key foundational portions of Scripture, and more. Discover how to apply God's word to your everyday life with the *NIV Young Women of Faith Bible.*

Hardcover 0-310-91394-2
Softcover 0-310-70278-X
Slate Leather–Look™ 0-310-70485-5
Periwinkle Leather–Look™ 0-310-70486-3

Available now at your local bookstore!

zonder**kidz**

Rough & Rugged Lily (Book 9)
Softcover 0-310-70260-7
The Year 'Round Holiday Book companion

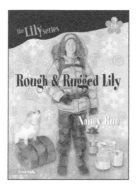

Lily Speaks! (Book 10)
Softcover 0-310-70262-3
The Values & Virtues Book companion

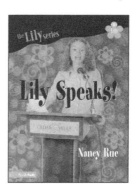

The Year 'Round Holiday Book ... It's a God Thing!
Softcover 0-310-70256-9
Rough & Rugged Lily companion

The Values & Virtues Book ... It's a God Thing!
Softcover 0-310-70257-7
Lily Speaks! companion

zonder**kidz**.

We want to hear from you. Please send your comments
about this book to us in care of zreview@zondervan.com. Thank you.

Grand Rapids, MI 49530
www.zonderkidz.com